100 IDEAS
for DADS who love their kids...

...but find them exhausting

100 IDEAS for DADS who love their kids...

...but find them exhausting

Willem van Eekelen

FEATHERSTONE
AN IMPRINT OF BLOOMSBURY
LONDON NEW DELHI NEW YORK SYDNEY

Many parents are almost permanently exhausted,
irritable and in borderline health.
Steve Biddulph

One study revealed that the vast majority
of parents don't like playing at all.
Tessa Livingstone

This book might help a bit.

Published 2014 by Featherstone Education
an imprint by Bloomsbury Publishing Plc
50 Bedford Square, London, WC1B 3DP
www.bloomsbury.com

Bloomsbury is a registered trademark of Bloomsbury Publishing Plc

ISBN 978-1-4729-0603-8

Text © Willem van Eekelen
Illustrations © Sarah Ray
Additional images © Shutterstock

Printed and bound in Great Britain by CPI Group (UK) Ltd, Croydon CR0 4YY

10 9 8 7 6 5 4 3 2 1

This book is produced using paper that is made from wood grown in
managed, sustainable forests. It is natural, renewable and recyclable.
The logging and manufacturing process conform to the
environmental regulations of the country of origin.

To see our full range of titles visit www.bloomsbury.com

CONTENTS

About this book

This book is for fathers,
grandfathers, carers and other
people with children in their lives.

Each suggestion has a rough age indicator
and all games can be played with
boys and girls alike (my use of 'he'
and 'she' is entirely random).

I hope you like the suggestions and
recognise their collective message:
with a bit of thought, games can
be exhilarating for children
and relaxing for adults!

Foreword

My GP asked me to make daily notes to see if my heartburn was stress-related. It was. I had heartburn on my days off. These were the days that I looked after my children.

I loved my son and daughter dearly (still do) but spending time with them exhausted me beyond belief. Until, one day, I challenged them to find games that required me to lie on the sofa.

It worked! I could be a fun and nurturing father without exerting much effort! I soon found out that this was possible in the car, the park, the pool, the forest – pretty much wherever parents and children spend time together. Within a week, my heartburn was gone.

Nurturing play requires no preparation or energy (or money). It's all a matter of game design. The key is to get your children to run around without running around yourself. To get them to think that household chores are fun. To keep them quietly entertained during long drives. To make them realise that for some games – like painting a penguin on your back – it is essential that you doze off.

Willem van Eekelen

A note on health and safety in this book

All games are safe as long as you keep allergies in mind, unless you are litigation-hungry, in which case all games are potentially dangerous and to be played with the utmost caution and at your own risk.

PART 1

IN AND AROUND THE HOUSE

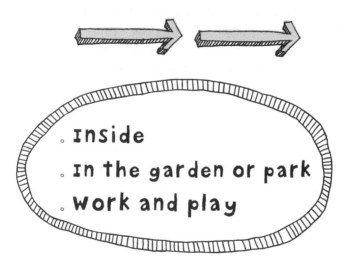

- Inside
- In the garden or park
- Work and play

Inside

Chilling out with your children is tricky, and even the most relaxing of situations can unexpectedly and suddenly turn into chaos. I wrote some of this chapter on the sofa, with my son next to me reading a book. My daughter was sitting across the room at the dining table, doing her homework. It was all very tranquil.

Occasionally, I would absentmindedly stroke my son's back. Then, unwittingly, one of my strokes was too much like a squeeze, and it tickled.
He threw his book in the air and attempted to tickle me back, with great force, giggling hysterically.
In what seemed to be a single leap from the dining table to the sofa, my daughter threw herself onto us – 'attaaaaaack!' – and tickled me with all her might.
I fell off the sofa, attacked by four small but fiery hands and knees.

Children are a frenzy waiting to happen.
Any moment, chaos may ensue. The suggestions in this chapter may increase your chances of a few blissfully quiet hours.

Ages 2-3 yrs

↑

This is a suggested age range. Don't take it too seriously.

The two extremes of peek-a-boo

For after a New Year fitness resolution:

Place your toddler in front of you when doing sit ups, or underneath you when doing push ups. Or lie on your back and use him as a weight: he'll love it. Don't do any toddler-lifting straight after your child has eaten *or he might throw up all over you*!

The rather less active version:
Lie down with a toddler on your chest and a handkerchief on your face. Take it off and put it on again in endless peek-a-boo repetition.

Mirror, mirror in the hand

Ages 2-4 yrs

Give your toddler a mirror and place her on your chest. Ask her to do things ('blow up your cheeks') or to make expressions ('look surprised').

One of two good things will happen: either you'll both end up making faces (which is fun), or she'll get absorbed by staring at her own image (which is nice and quiet).

Keep on rolling

Ages 2–5 yrs

Sit on the floor, legs apart, with your child a few feet away, rolling a ball back and forth. This game requires very little concentration and the steadily rolling ball has a somewhat hypnotic effect – maybe that's why the game often causes introverted children to open up.

The not-so-white wall behind the door

Ages 2 onwards

Choose an inconspicuous part of the wall. Then, every 6 months or so, ask your child to stand straight against it, and mark his or her length with a dash and a date. The beautiful thing is that every new measurement is an achievement – 'look, you grew!' – as children tend to get taller over time.

Talk to the hand

Ages 2–6 yrs

For when you're on the sofa:

Put on a hand puppet and drop another one on the floor next to you. Children find this curious and inspiring, and the chances are that they will take the other puppet and you'll end up having a really nice time and a quiet puppet conversation. You might even learn a thing or two, as puppets sometimes cushion a child's embarrassment about something else that is going on. This is how a friend of mine found out about his son's constipation.

On puppets

Child therapists often use puppets, as they make things less confrontational. Puppets do more than just aid conversations. My sister's sons played games through their puppets for a while. This made losing less painful, as it was no longer the *boy* who lost, but the *puppet*. The brothers even started to give each other's puppet advice.

Get yourself drawn

Ages 2–6 yrs

If you've got some leftover wallpaper, lie on it and let your loved ones outline you. Alternatively, sit down with an A4 sheet under your feet, or under your hands on the table.

Another possibility:
Sit in your favourite chair, take your reading-the-paper position and check where the reading light casts your shadow on the wall. That's where you stick a piece of paper for your child to draw your profile on. Only attempt this with older children if you treasure a clean wall!

Ages 2–6 yrs

His first record

This is another game I used to play with my child on my chest. Record the songs he sings, and listen to them together. You could also play a song on your phone and ask him to dance to it.

what's *that!?*

Give your child a spoon and
ask her to tap it against various things.
You then close your eyes and guess what she is tapping
it against. Another version: ask her to give you objects,
and guess what they are while keeping your eyes closed.
Take your time and say ridiculous things ('it's an ele-
phant!'). The easiest way to turn the tables is to throw,
say, your child's plastic animal collection into a bag or
bucket, and ask her to close her eyes and find the horse.

If your children are young, limit the number of things,
and show them each item before you place it in
the bag.

Pillow fun

Give each of your children a soft pillow
and challenge them to knock you off
your armchair. Close your eyes and enjoy
the softness of the pillows and the children's ever-
increasing excitement. Occasionally express your 'agony'.
After a while, fall slowly on to the floor, moaning gently
like a cowboy in the movies.

Older children continue to find this an exhilarating
challenge, but their growing muscle power renders
the game increasingly less relaxing.

The two extremes of ballooning

Lie on the bed and hit a balloon in all directions while the children run around in attempts to hit it back to you. If you want a competitive element, say that the balloon isn't allowed to bounce on the ground.

If you're willing to sit up, you could introduce a second competitive element, where you lose if the balloon bounces on the bed.

Lost control

Five slow-down principles

Principle	Example
1. Use slow toys	Slow any ball game down by replacing the ball with a balloon.
2. Use slow rules	Any guessing or riddle game can be slowed down if you guess in turn instead of all together (see 'When travelling' p.44-49 for examples of such games).
3. Simulate movement	When dancing, for example, you can work yourself into a sweat, but you can also hold two scarves and simulate a great deal of movement simply by flipping your hands.
4. Minimise movement	When chasing children you can run after them, but you can also merely growl, stick out your hands and take a step or two. They'll flee screaming, but then creep back to you, hoping for a new scare.
5. Complicate movement	Playing catch is not quite as fast when children play it with a book on their head or a ping-pong ball on a spoon.

Be a statue

Ages 3-10 yrs

In turn, you sit or stand in whatever way, and the child guesses what you are. If you feel energetic, go for things such as 'a tennis player' and 'a marathon runner'. If not, go for 'somebody who is reading a book', 'somebody who is asleep' and 'somebody who thinks'. You could also act things out (frying an egg, getting dressed) or play the animal version of this game (guess who, in our house, played the sloth and the hedgehog?).

Relax together

Ages 3-10 yrs

'I'm trying something new – would you like to join me? Lie down next to me. I'm discovering all my muscles, and relaxing them. Are you ready? OK, feet first: try to totally relax your feet.' If your children are as gullible as mine, you'll spend at least 20 minutes on your back, gradually relaxing muscles from your feet to your skull. An added advantage might be that your children get to know the names of body parts.

You, the model

Ages 4-10 yrs

For when it's all quiet and calm but you notice that your child is looking for something new: 'Could you draw a picture of me, please?' And then you continue with what you're doing, or gently chat away as she works.

The challenge

Ask, in wonderment, if your child is able to do X, Y or Z.
For example:

- 'Hey, I was wondering if you were able to walk all the way across the room and back with this book on your head?... Wooowww!... And are you able to do it while walking backwards, too?'
- 'My goodness, you have so much energy! Do you ever get tired? But I'm sure you aren't able to climb the stairs and back seven times! Are you?'
- 'I'd love to know the length of this room, and you are one metre tall. Could you check how many times you fit in the length of this room, please?'

Anything goes, most things only work once, and much depends on the child's age.

Ages 3–10 yrs

Ages 3–5 yrs

Driving around in your chair

Your chair or sofa is the taxi and the child on your lap is the driver. You give a bit of initial input ('could you drive me to the zoo please?') and then give your child the imaginary steering wheel.

I first tried a bus version, but it was not quite as relaxing as my son made me step in and out a lot.

Rediscover your identity

This is for when you don't want to get up in the morning but your child has appeared and is ready for action. 'Hello girl / boy, I slept really well but now I can't remember who I am. Can you help me please?' To rediscover your identity you ask questions about yourself and about your child. You listen to the answers with your eyes closed as this helps you to concentrate (not for snorers). The answers might be sobering. 'What kind of work do I do?' 'You always play on your computer.'

Willem's words of wisdom

A standard recommendation in books about raising kids is that you allow them to take charge of the way games takes shape. Unfortunately, most games designed by young children are simultaneously tiring and intensely boring, and often lack a recognisable aim or end product (which is something that fathers tend to need to remain happy).

Don't go there when you're even just the tiniest bit tired and don't believe parents who say that time flies when they are with their children. It doesn't. Two hours of real play – even of the type covered in this book – is a loooong time.

Beauty parlour

Play beauty parlour and you'll find that young children find faces fascinating. If you let them, there will be a great deal of investigative prodding and poking (beware of your eyes). Cucumber slices, whatever cream (I recall using toothpaste), peanut butter, shaving gel – it can all be spread around on your face.

Your hair or, if you're completely bald, your skull, is of interest too.

Remove ribbons before leaving the house.

Find it

Hide a number of small items (you might want to make a little list, if your memory isn't the strongest) and ask your child to find them. You may want to play this game when you want to tidy the house, as the inevitable next step is that your child hides things that you have to find – which is a rather pleasant addition to tidying up. Coach them a bit, the first time they do this, just to avoid coins being hidden in the DVD player.

Sticking to your marbles

Ages
5-10 yrs

All conventional games with marbles involve a lot of standing around. Not this one. Each player gets an equal number of Playmobil or Lego figures, or anything else that can stand and won't break, and places them in front of him or herself. Then, in turn, roll a marble towards your opponent's figures. The last one with standing figures wins. Your legs are the funnel that catches the marble, which means that you very rarely have to get up. For very young children, tennis balls might work better.

My very cool uncle Titus taught me a one-sided version of this game when I was ten years old and temporarily bed-bound. He would rest his back against the wall and forever roll the marble back to me while I tried to knock down his Lego-men. It's one of my best childhood memories, generated in one of my worst childhood weeks.

The actor and the scriptwriter

You are the scriptwriter. You take your position on the sofa and introduce the character. Your child becomes the character and goes wherever your story takes her.

Children don't always need a coherent story line and it's totally possible to incorporate exercise ('suddenly, she explodes into a frantic dance') or small tasks ('with a look of shock and horror, Bellatrix takes three plates from the cupboard and places them on the table; then she adds the cutlery.').

Beware of the risk of reversal: the moment may come where your child insists on making up the play, and on you acting it out. Her play is likely to involve chases and heavy lifting.

Lip reading

Sit at some distance from each other. In turn, say things without sound and guess what the other is saying. Things like 'I love you' are easy, but with a bit of practice it's possible to get your child to understand things such as 'touch your nose'.

Ever-so-slightly less relaxed, but very enjoyable, are the versions where you use non-verbal signs or facial and bodily expressions, or act out situations. No child remains passive when you give a good 'I-really-need-to-go-to-the-toilet-*now*' performance.

Ages
6-10 yrs

When the house had to be really quiet, my mother would bake a cake. We loved cakes and were told that even the slightest of noises would cause it to implode. It caused us to tiptoe around the house. No cake ever imploded.

Treasure hunt

Ages 6–10 yrs

Treasure hunts require you to produce and hide a series of clues, such as 'Look between the plates.' The clues lead the children to an end point, where they may find a sweet or piece of chocolate. Treasure hunts require some preparation but have three advantages, in addition to being fun.

1. You can prepare for them when you have time, and tell your children about them whenever it suits you.

2. It is possible to integrate minor useful activities in the instructions ('empty the dishwasher; you'll find the next instruction while doing so' – and then hide an instruction in, say, the cutlery drawer).

3. Children are likely to reciprocate and spend a long time preparing a treasure hunt for you.

Explicitly capping questions

Sometimes you want to watch a movie together but your child keeps interrupting with questions. The solution: announce, right at the start, that he is allowed to ask ten questions in total.
This has two advantages:

- Because the number of questions is limited, it's much easier to snap out of the movie in order to give meaningful answers. I no longer try to answer questions without pausing the movie – which is good, as this never really worked.

- Children choose their questions carefully as they don't want to run out of them. No maximum limit leads to a hundred questions, but a maximum of ten generally limits the questions to five or less.

I use the same quota system when working. 'You can disturb me five times in the coming hour, OK?'
My daughter introduced an extra safety check by always starting every such engagement with a three-step procedure:

1. 'Papa, I want to say something. Focus.'
2. She gives me a moment and then checks: 'Are you focused?'
3. I actually focus, nod meekly, and she starts.
   I can't believe I'm admitting this, but it really helps me. When working and without her instruction to focus, I often found myself only lending her half an ear.

Tying you down

You read the paper while the children use towels, sheets or other soft things to tie you up. Young children can spend forever trying but will never be able to actually tie you up. Children appreciate the occasional show ('oh no, I can't get out of this chair!').
Don't use ropes that might hurt you.

Mummification

In the garden or park

It is so nice to spend time outside. On high-energy days, go play football, run together, play tag. For all other days, you might want to take a look at this chapter's suggestions.

They're all good weather suggestions for in the garden or nearby park. I have tried and tried but not found relaxing games to play in rainy weather. When it rains, we go outside and run through and stamp in puddles, catch raindrops with our mouths and get soaking wet – and then have a relaxing time drinking hot chocolate in dry clothes, sitting next to the radiator.

It's the same with snow: I can't think of anything you could do without it being cold and energy-consuming, and the things that keep me going are the fun and the prospect of a hot drink. This chapter, therefore, is incomplete. For a more comprehensive next edition of this book, I hope that you'll send your bad-weather suggestions to: willem@totallychilledoutparenting.com

Retrieving the ball

This is the game people play with their
dog. Small children totally dig it.

The soap bubble version of this game gets children all
giggly and running around hysterically, while you remain
seated. You take your kids' refillable bubble blower and ask
them to collect the bubbles you blow, and return them to
you. It can't be done – but it's forever fun trying. Don't spill
the contents of the bottle on the grass, or the grass will die.

Willem's words of wisdom

Different balls have different speeds.
If you play something where *you* will run
after the ball, use a slow non-bouncy ball like
a softball, bean ball, balloon, beach ball, foam
ball, rolled-up sock or a wet sponge on a warm day.
If *your children* are the ones who will be running
after the ball, use a fast bouncy ball like a football,
tennis ball or rubber ball. Beware of the Frisbee:
it doesn't bounce but has an uncanny ability
to roll further and further away from you.

fast....   ....slow

Ages
2-7 yrs

Wrestling

You are stronger than your children and leg muscles are much stronger than arm muscles. If you lie in the grass and squeeze a football between your legs with the challenge to free it (protect your privates) then the children totally exhaust themselves while you barely notice the need to tighten your muscles. This kind of game works with anything small in your hand too: somehow, it's much easier to clench than to unclench fingers.

Getting wet not getting wet

Ages
2-10 yrs

When watering the garden on a warm day: let the children try to run through the stream without getting wet – they'll love it.

Ages
3-7 yrs

Animal farm

Place plastic animals in the corners of the garden, to represent animal groups such as birds, mammals, insects and fish. You then sit in the middle of the garden and instruct the children to go from one corner to the next. In the beginning, children just 'go to birds!', but after a while you ask them to 'swim to the fish!' or 'skip backwards to mammals!' Yet later you trick them: 'tiptoe to the insects' while pointing to the fish.

Wise old fool

Invite your children to look for and
bring you things that they want to know
more about – grasses, leaves, flowers etc.
Sometimes, this works as planned: you relax while they're
searching and then respond as the wise father. 'Ah, this is
an oak nut. Squirrels eat oak nuts. They bury them for the
winter but sometimes forget the location – and this might
be the beginning of a new oak tree.'

For urban nerds, the more common and rather
less honourable option is to admit that you don't have
the faintest idea. Once children see a pattern of ignorance,
they tend to find this quite delightful and will work hard
to find other unidentifiable objects. Also nice but slightly
more demanding: make up nonsense. 'Ah, this looks like
the poo of a flying horse. Could you soak it in a glass of
water please, and then we can check tomorrow if it has
turned pink?'

If you have a particularly good nose you might
want to try the smells version of this game.
This allows you to keep your eyes closed.

Stop and go

Children go from A to B in a manner
dictated by you, and stop when you
say 'stop!'. 'Backwards on your toes,' 'walk on
hands and feet,' 'sing like a bird while crawling' (and enjoy
the sudden silence after 'stop!') – there are a thousand
possibilities. It's an extended version of the Red-Light-
Green-Light running game, really.

what do you hear?

Ages 3-10 yrs

'Hey, come and lie next to me.
I thought it was totally quiet here, but
I'm starting to hear all sorts of sounds. Shall we
list the things we hear? I'll go first: I hear a bird sing.
Now you: what do you hear?'

What do you see?

'Hey, come and lie next to me. I'm looking at the
clouds and I see all sorts of shapes. I can see a face
– can you find it? And what else do you see?'

Ages 3-10 yrs

Ages 3-10 yrs

Bird of paradise

Ask the children to collect different
things – rocks, leaves, flowers – and
then make some sort of bird of paradise
exhibition with it. Or a zoo-in-a-jar,
if your children are more into snails,
ants, ladybirds, worms and spiders.

Paint stuff

Ages 4-5 yrs

'Could you paint a blue circle on that tree
trunk / your face on that wall / one of that
tree's leaves yellow please?' If you position
your chair carefully, you won't have to move at all.

Tasks

Children love playful tasks and will forever return for another one. At four, the tasks are simple. 'Give that tree a hug and come back.' 'Lie down and roll yourself to the daffodils.' Later on, the tasks become more complex and need a purpose. 'Get me ten daisies from the top of the hill, so that we can make a daisy chain.' 'Dribble the ball around those five trees, to improve your ball control.'

Detecting movement (A version of Grandmother's Footsteps)

Lie in a field and ask the children to take 50 large steps away from you. When you say 'Start' they have to approach you, but so quietly that you can't hear a thing. Whenever you (pretend to) hear anything, you open your eyes and tilt your head towards the children – the sign for the children to instantly freeze. If you see a child move, you shriek ('Mary, I saw you move!'). They win when they manage to touch you without having been caught moving, or without having been caught more than a few times. It's a real thrill for children, and it requires nothing from you except for a celebration at the end.

Stationary hula-hoop

Ages
5-7 yrs

I thought of this when my daughter was in her hula-hoop stage and insisted we did it together. It uses much less energy than actual hula-hooping, but you need a stretch of at least five metres. This is how it works:

You stand and throw the hula-hoop with a lot of backspin (as you do with bowls). This causes the hoop to jump forwards, quickly slow down, and return to you. Your child's objective is to catch it before it returns to you. Once you've got the hang of it, you'll see that you don't move much, while your child is running all over the place.

Ages
5-10 yrs

Fast, faster, fastest

Anything can be timed or counted. My most common task is along the lines of 'please touch all lamp posts on the square / trees in this garden / fences on this playground, and run back to me!'

Whatever the task: repeat it a few times and confirm progress ('Great, this time it was only 23 seconds – you're getting better and better!') It's easy to break records as you don't use a watch: just pretend you are counting.

where's my shoe?

Make the children look up ('look – is that the Batmobile?!') and quickly throw away your shoes. 'Oh no, I've accidentally thrown my shoes away!'

You are now demobilised, so you sit down while they find and return your shoes. With a bit of luck they'll see the humour and want you to repeat it many times.

Note the slight risk of losing a shoe. Another risk: Mike, a friend who tested this game for me, reported back that his children didn't play along and that he ended up tottering around in his socks, in search of his shoes and feeling rather less than entirely relaxed.

Willem's words of wisdom

Only give in to the impulse to throw Max high into the air when you have loads of energy. You will end up having to do it a number of times with Max and with Lily and with all other children in the neighbourhood, and to endure all the overexcited children you'll inevitably end up with.

Work and play

Children are oblivious to the fact that you have a life of your own. My son wanted to text me his lunch box preference during his school's morning break, which I could then prepare and deliver.

My daughter suggested that I come to school at the end of the day, so that she could then choose between walking and being driven home. Yeah, right. When in the greatest of hurries, requests for homework support / making eggs / playing Monopoly cause me to give – let me phrase it mildly – uncharitable responses. Similarly, when focused on the children, attempts to quickly do something useful have led to shrunk clothes and emails that, on reflection, I would much rather not have sent.

At other times, a combination of work and play is possible. Playing tag takes all my attention, but I get many household chores done while playing hide-and-seek. As it turns out, I can talk and make jokes while washing the dishes, but attempts to wash the dishes while my daughter is making pancakes causes a level of distraction that makes me break things.

Books on childrearing tell you that children can help you with your chores, or even do them independently.

This is true. Young children can set the table, empty the dishwasher (if you are prepared to sacrifice a few plates), vacuum clean and prepare simple meals. They often love to mow the grass, wash the dog (coach them carefully) and solve your computer problems (a field in which they'll probably outperform you by the age of eight). However, I would like to add three rules.

Firstly, think of timing and importance. When in the kitchen, don't make your progress dependent on his progress. This means a 'no' to him washing the pan you need or getting the ingredients out of the fridge, and a 'yes' to him adding strawberries to the yoghurt and preparing the salad.

Secondly, think of the damage they could potentially cause. My son has done unspeakable things when painting a wall, but it's behind a bookshelf so it doesn't really matter. In the same trusting manner, I welcomed his support when there was ice on the car. I so wish I had provided a mock alternative, with me de-icing the car while he de-iced his tricycle...

Thirdly, don't get your hopes up. Most young children are keen to help, but this desire disappears the moment they are old or skilled enough to actually be useful.

It's all about incentives

I used to walk my children to school.
Oh, the stress of the daily struggle to leave on time!
Games like 'let's pretend we're fast flying planes!'
didn't work. Attempts to intimidate by counting
('I'll count to three now: oooone...') meant nothing
to them. Pleas for compassion ('I'm going to have a heart
attack because of this!') made no difference at all.

Then, one day, I found the solution: I tripled
my children's pocket money, provided that they had
been ready and outside by 8 o'clock sharp, every day of
the preceding week. This changed everything immediately.

They were never late. Initially, I felt bad about bribing my kids
into good behaviour. Then I rephrased it into 'rewarding
my kids for good behaviour' and my conscience was clear.

Maarten, my brother-in-law, solved a similar problem.
His daughter used to get upset whenever he was not
waiting at the gate when she finished school. He introduced
a reward system: five minutes late meant pancakes,
and ten minutes late meant chips.
No more red and angry faces: Ida now
hopes that Maarten is late!

The laundry puzzle

Ages
3–7 yrs

Young children can't do or hang washing properly, but have a surprising ability to find the matching socks and to sort clothes by person. Your chances of them liking it increase if you present it as a puzzle. Nowadays, I throw it all on the bed, add all the socks from my single-sock-bag, and we make this 'puzzle' together.

Another puzzle: 'which items in this room do not belong in this room?' Your child identifies them, puts them all into a basket, and distributes them to their rightful place.

Do as I do

Ages
3–5 yrs

'Follow me, and do what I do.' Then go and do your things, with the toddler behind you pretending to do the same. It's quite a lot of fun. I particularly treasure the memory of my daughter and me shaving in the morning – she with a lot of foam and a spoon.

Spoon-shaving

Willem's words of wisdom

Many by-products of chores serve as a useful distraction for the children. If you let them, kids will turn freshly cut grass into a grass castle, dough into clay and flour into hands prints. Piles of clothes means dressing up.

Best of all: when changing the bed linen, kids really enjoy sitting quietly underneath a growing pile of it. Be amazed that they have disappeared, even though they were there a second ago, and you'll see the pile gently shake with silent giggles.

Write it all down, please

This is for pre-schoolers who like to pretend they're writing. Give your child a notebook and ask her to follow you around the house and make notes about what you're doing. We used to do this 'for the benefit of later generations,' but you probably won't need to give a reason.

Because you know what chores you've done it is easy to review the 'text' and read it out loud. Once the child has learned how to write, this is no longer interesting.

Ages
4–5 yrs

Tidying rooms while lying down with your eyes closed

Tell your son that you've read that children see better in the dark than adults (which I heard is true) and that you don't believe it. Suggest testing it out. Then take a quick look at the mess in his room, switch off the light, emphasise that you can't see a thing, and lie on the bed with your eyes closed. Ask him to find all Lego / laundry / magazines and place them in the box / in the laundry basket / on the pile. When you can't think of anything else, ask if there's anything left on the floor – and get it cleared. Turn the light back on and be amazed. If your own room is messy too, go there and repeat.

Next time the room is a mess, you suddenly realise that it's easier to recognise shapes than colours, and you wonder if your child may be able to tidy all yellow / green / blue things. Switch off the lights, lie down, close your eyes, and conduct the colour-based tidying test.

Have your picture taken

'I need a number of really good pictures of me cleaning the house to impress Mum. Could you follow me and take some please?' You no longer feel the pressure to stop cleaning to play with your child. Instead, you continue cleaning your house while playing with your child at the same time.

Hide-and-seek and do some work

Ages
4-10 yrs

Follow the three golden rules and you will get some work done:

1. Never agree to count out loud. If you agree to it once, you'll forever lose the possibility to do something that requires thinking while pretending to be counting. Most children will not need more than '25...50...75...90...100.'

2. Find yourself comfortable hiding places and take your laptop with you. I wrote the first bits of this book in the cupboard under the stairs.

3. If your child goes into hiding and you could hear which room she went to, then go to another part first to tidy things up, and make the occasional noise or disappointed grunt. 'Oh no, she's not in the kitchen either!'

Hide and seek and work

40

Two golden rules

1. When your children want to leave the house and you wonder if you could quickly do a chore before they are ready to go, the answer is yes. You can do a quick chore and a few other things too, as your children won't be ready any time soon. They get distracted. I often use this golden rule when I need to finish something. 'Sure, sweetheart, I'm ready whenever you have your shoes and coat on' – and I generally have another 20 minutes before she reappears.

2. When you want to leave the house and you wonder if *your children* could quickly do something – anything – before leaving the house, the answer is no. It will take much longer than you think, and you will get stressed out.

PART 2
OUT AND ABOUT

- when travelling
- when stuck
- in the forest
- on the beach
- in the pool

When travelling

Ah, out and about. This is the place where children run off and get lost. This is where your response to tantrums is evaluated by people you know and by people you don't. This is where I cleaned my toddler son's bottom with a sandy beach towel because I'd forgotten the wipes, sweating in 40 degrees with my daughter standing next to me whining and a hundred beachgoers judging me from the bus that we were about to miss. Out and about is where I carried, more than once, my two exhausted children for what felt like miles to a car I couldn't find. I have regularly returned from out and about feeling defeated and deflated.

Out and about is also where the best childhood memories take shape. It's where children make their friends and where they release loads of energy. It's where they learn quickly and effortlessly. Out and about is the spice of life. It's a mixed bag, but when it's good it's great, which is why people go there.

Willem's words of wisdom

On long drives we used to sing songs, which creates a great deal of noise in a very small space. We also played memory games (which requires continuous concentration) and cards (imagine the back ache after an hour of blackjack). No longer. Nowadays, we do the rather more relaxing things described in the next few pages.

Discuss your work

Ages 2-10 yrs

This might not work for everybody, but it works well for us: I ask my children to help me solve a work-related problem ('Why do I never find time to take a lunch break?' 'Why do meetings always take longer than necessary?'). I present the problem in detail and ask for their advice. Perhaps the unusually serious intonation causes children to listen quietly. In the earlier years, I never really got any meaningful feedback, but the need to present the issues with child-friendly coherence did help me to order my thoughts on the matter.

Unexpectedly, these sessions are amongst the childhood memories my daughter recounts most fondly. I think she enjoyed the honour of being part of Daddy's adult world.

I spy

Ages 3-10 yrs

Find something. A yellow car, a motorcycle, a house, a caravan, a dog – the rarer the object, the longer it's quiet (but not with very young children – they'll get impatient). The one who sees it first wins. You're the driver so you rarely win, and this makes the game all the more attractive for the children.

Awake the animal inside you

Ages 3-6 yrs

In turn, make the sound of an animal. The others guess what animal it is. It's a relaxed but somewhat frustrating game, unless you know a lot of sounds. For some, simply describing an animal works better than sounding like one.

What's the word, hummingbird?

Ages 4-10 yrs

Take a word and find words that rhyme with it. By taking turns, you avoid it turning into a high-speed competition.

Once the children get older you might want to start with thematic words (like car parts) or jointly build poems instead of merely listing words that rhyme.

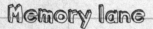

Ages 4-10 yrs

Memory lane

In turn, recount a fond memory. 'Ah, remember when we always fed the ducks at the weekend?' Children as young as four love playing this game, as they like talking about 'when they were small'.

Long car journeys are particularly likely to turn 'Memory lane' into long conversations. Maybe it's because you do not actually look at each other, or maybe it's the motion. Whatever it is: people get to know their children (and their parents) better in the course of lengthy car rides.

Counting the minutes

They close their eyes at 5, 4, 3, 2, 1, *now*, and count one minute in their heads. They say '60' when their minute is over, and the one closest to the actual minute wins. Ah, blissful silence... you'll want to give a lot of revenge opportunities. My friend Suzanne turned the rules around and plays it in the morning, in bed and with her eyes closed, trying to estimate five minutes while her daughter Sarima keeps an eye on the stopwatch.

Ages 7-10 yrs

Guess what I'm thinking of

Yes/no questions get the other person closer and closer to the answer. With small children, the game is simple ('guess what animal I'm thinking of'), but as they grow older they'll want more complexity. By the age of ten, many children can handle pretty much anything – our last five answers were 'yellow,' 'water vapour,' 'the universe,' 'badminton' and the word 'light-hearted'.

You could also reverse the game by introducing words that don't exist and getting each other to find the meaning through yes/no questions. Start easy ('blall' means a blue ball) and see how complex you can make it ('zabam' means 'getting a camel into motion by whistling').

'Guess who I'm thinking off' also works.

Before you suggest trying to imitate each others' weirdest noises and faces: think of how far your children will drag you outside of your comfort zone if they want to play this in a crowded train!

Willem's words of wisdom

An investment that vastly improved the quality of a few of our long car journeys – the spray that cleans seats after a child has thrown up all over it. Before we knew this spray existed, we occasionally had to choose between the stench of vomit and the freezing winds of winter. After a tip from a friend, vomiting formed merely a minor hold-up.

Secret languages

Ages
5–10 yrs

Make a sentence in a secret language and wonder if the children can figure out what you're saying. For example:

- Add 'ip' to every word: lip wantip someip sweetsip.

- Start every word with 'mo' and end it with 'ip': Mo-lip mowantip mosomeip mosweetsip.

- Turn the words around: Sweets some want I.

Once they've deciphered it, with or without your help, invite the children to make sentences for you to translate. The more complex the language, the longer it'll take for the children to prepare sentences. You don't have to get it at once: the children will enjoy your quietness and confused mumblings ('… I want… some… what? Again please!').

If you and your children are particularly talented you might want to try spoonerisms too. This is where you swap letters: I swant some weets. Or – no particular talent required – make weird sounds and ask the children to repeat them.

Ages
6–10 yrs

Number plates

Read the number plates of the cars around you and ask the children to make words or funny sentences out of the letters. 'AEL?' 'Absolutely Enormous Lettuce!' Once they get the hang of it, it's possible to follow themes ('and now it's got to do with sports').

Anchovies, Brussels sprouts, cabbage (food kids don't like, alphabetically)

Ages 3-5 yrs

Nearly every theme can be used for the alphabet game. Animals, names of countries, things in the kitchen, girl/boy names, 'all things British', food, drinks, 'things you see while driving': it all works. The only version that failed miserably, in our family, is the one where the next person needs to find a word with one more syllable than the word mentioned before (as in app, apple, apartment, apparition, aphrodisiac, anthropological, apologetically). It made my children cry.

Keep in mind that:

• Saying words in turn is more relaxing than 'being the quickest.'

• When it's your turn: take your time. Nobody likes the game any better if you always have your word ready right away.

• If you each say an animal that starts with an A and then move to B, it may turn out to be a rather high-speed game. You slow down the game considerably if you continue with each letter until there are no more animals that start with that letter, and only then move to the next one.

What's her life like?

Ages 4-10 yrs

Drive by a car and take a quick look at the driver. Discuss: where is she going to and why? What's she like, and what life has she lived so far? Once children get into this, they'll make up all sorts of stuff. A friend of mine gives these drivers names, and then plays the memory game of 'I drove to London and saw... Lady Longhair, Sir Sternface, ...'

When stuck

Take any kind of delay as lightly as you possibly can as the general rule is that, when stuck anywhere, the children will mirror your mood.

These suggestions might help to pass the time. Parts of the chapter 'When travelling' also work when you're stuck – like the rhyming game and 'Memory lane'.

Note that you and your children have different ideas of what 'being stuck' means. For most children sitting in a restaurant, for example, is effectively 'being stuck.'

Willem's words of wisdom

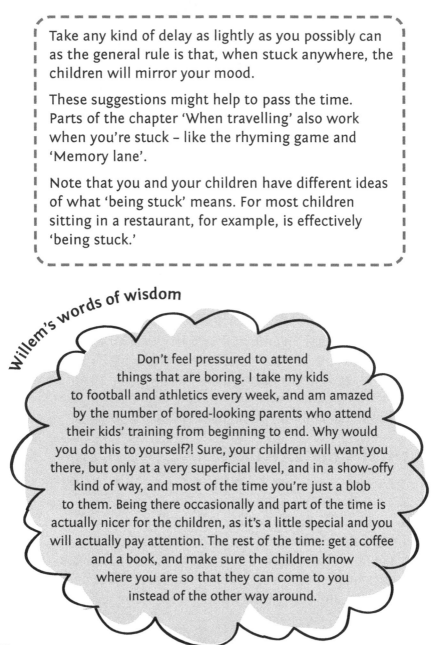

Don't feel pressured to attend things that are boring. I take my kids to football and athletics every week, and am amazed by the number of bored-looking parents who attend their kids' training from beginning to end. Why would you do this to yourself?! Sure, your children will want you there, but only at a very superficial level, and in a show-offy kind of way, and most of the time you're just a blob to them. Being there occasionally and part of the time is actually nicer for the children, as it's a little special and you will actually pay attention. The rest of the time: get a coffee and a book, and make sure the children know where you are so that they can come to you instead of the other way around.

Drawing-when-stuck

Once, my friend John had to wait for hours in a hospital, with two small children and he was entirely unprepared. The receptionist lent him a pen and a piece of paper, and the three of them created a detailed drawing – a house with a forest and lake – by passing the piece of paper around, each adding a single line every time. Something that could have gone so wrong ended up being a very nice and quiet day with the children.

If you have more than a single piece of paper, and the children are not so very young, you could take turns to draw:
• A head and fold the page head-down
• An upper body and fold the page body-down
• The legs and fold the page legs-down
• The feet and see what monster you've jointly created.

With each transfer, make sure that the tips of the previous bit remain visible, so that the end result is a drawing with four strange but connected parts.

Writing-when-stuck

In turn, you write a line and pass the story on to the next person. It's also possible to do this verbally, but it tends to be a lot louder and quicker, and thus much more energy-consuming. When children are losing interest you could introduce a new dimension: folding the page after every line, which makes the stories even more bizarre.

Know your inner elbow

Take your child's hand and gently tickle her palm. Ask her to close her eyes and very slowly (*very* slowly, or it won't work) tickle upwards. Ask her to open her eyes when she thinks that you have reached her inner elbow. For reasons I don't know, people young and old think this moment has come long before it actually comes – sometimes you're barely half-way. After a while you'll see a learning curve, and that's the moment you switch roles.

I first played this little game at home. This is not quite as relaxing. The thing is: when you're stuck somewhere, there is an external environment in which the children feel minor social inhibitions, causing them to enjoy the game quietly. At home there are no such inhibitions, and the game is likely to deteriorate into a screaming tickling contest.

Follow me blindly

Take turns to draw something - a pond, a duck, a tree - with your eyes closed.

For talented artists: ask them to draw something with several components and laugh at the end result (for example: a house with a pond, with a duck in and a tree next to it).

Also nice: in turn, draw something with your eyes closed and let the others guess what it is meant to be.

Are you going to attend an important event that your children might interpret as 'being stuck'? Giving them a large lollipop, or anything else that is very attractive, keeps them busy and does not make noise. Make them think that the event is essentially about this lollipop.

This is how I got my children to sit through a wedding without a sound, for example. 'And then we'll go into that room and while Tina is getting married you will be eating that giant lollipop!'

TICKET NO: 00000007
KIOSK C →

In the forest

Introduction

Up until my children were 8 or so, they found the next few activities entertaining. After that, they decided that forests were boring. For a while, I could persuade them by rephrasing the proposal from 'a nature walk' to 'picking berries' and 'eating ice cream in the forest café' but this didn't last long. I really miss it, and hope you're luckier. If you, too, have to resort to the 'berry' excuse: make sure they wear long clothes to protect them from the thorns and put most of *your* berries in *their* containers. It might extend their enthusiasm for another year.

Building a dam is tiring.

Floating down the river

Whenever you find a stream that does not flow too fast: everybody selects a stick and throws it in the water. Then stroll downstream and sit down somewhere, waiting for the sticks to show up. If you're a competitive bunch, the stick that arrives first is the winner.

Forest soup

Suggest to your children that you are going to make forest soup: 'Sweetheart, let's make soup when we're home. Could you collect the ingredients please? I need three acorns, five dandelions, two daisies, four small pebbles and a chestnut.' You might want to write down ingredients before you leave, in case your children find a written list more persuasive than a verbal list.

You don't have to make soup. You could also play restaurants, shops, have a tea party, make a treasure box or clean and then paint a few rocks or pines. It all serves the same purpose: it keeps the children entertained during a forest walk and enthusiastic at the prospect of further play once you're home.

Make sure they stay away from mushrooms. If there are rare things in the forest: ask your children to find them but not take them without your approval. If you are unsure about what's protected and what's not: you could make a photo-based version of the game ('could you get me a picture of a flower, a bird and a mushroom please?').

Ages
5-7 yrs

Find the leaf

Collect a few leaves in the course of your walk, and put them in your pocket. After a while, produce them one by one and ask the children to find a look-alike sibling for each of them. Another option: 'could you find me ten different types of leaves please?'

It is during this game that I learned that rewards potentially ruin a game. I once suggested that every new type of leaf was ten pence towards the ice cream we were going to eat. From that moment onwards, this was no longer a game but something that required a reward. I also learned that there are a lot of different leaves in the forest, and that they jointly amount to a tower of ice cream with cream and sprinkles and chocolate sauce.

Willem's words of wisdom

With young children, fun nature walks have to be ridiculously short, or you'll end up carrying them.

Kicking it

Walk while jointly kicking a pebble or pine nut (or, in the case of my daughter, a bottle lid that she kept especially for this purpose). It helps with the last mile in particular, when children tend to slow down to a speed that tests your patience. You can kick pebbles with younger children too, but it won't be as relaxing as they do not yet have the skills.

Willem's words of wisdom

When the children were smaller, I was a bit nervous about losing them. I kept them close to me by explaining that I liked nature walks so much that I sometimes forgot that I had company, and wandered off. Could they please keep an eye on me? Yes they could, and they did, and they found it hilarious whenever I pretended to be walking off the track with an absent-minded look on my face.

On the beach

The beach is so much better in quiet hours
or in a quiet area. It reduces the risk of you losing
a child in the crowd, which I know (first-hand, alas)
is one of the most stressful things a parent can
experience. You may want to write your phone
number on your child's arm, just in case.

King of the castle

Ages
2–10 yrs

It's really nice to make sandcastles.
Sometimes, it's even nicer to be part of one.
Make sure your body rests comfortably as you'll be
lying still for quite a while. If you have the type of body
that starts aching when it lies still: this one is not for you.
I personally like it better when I sit instead of lie down,
partly because a lying position makes the occasional
refreshment harder to drink. If you're truly comfy, it's
possible to extend the game forever ('and could you
put some shells on me please, in the shape of fish?').

Ages
4–6 yrs

Retreat!

Stand at the edge of the tide.
In between two waves you yell 'Go!' and
the children run towards the sea; when
a new wave appears you yell 'Retreat!'
and the children run back to
the safety of your arms.

Shadowy figures

Ages 4-10 yrs

Sit down if you must, or stand in a pose if you can (as the shape will be clearer) and ask your child to mark your shadow. Get them to decorate it with shells.

Ages 2-10 yrs

Shapely bums

You all sit in the wet sand, at the edge of the sea. Take your time, and all wriggle a bit to make deep imprints of your bottoms. Then watch the mighty force of the sea: how many waves does it take for the imprints to disappear?

Shapely bums don't last forever

In the pool

Like most parents, I've found that holidays with children ideally feature a swimming pool. Like most parents, I tend to divide pool time between fun but tiring games with the children, and relaxing while the children entertain themselves. After years in pools, I have found only very few ways to chill-with-kids.

The pool paradox

Ages 2-4 yrs

The pool paradox is that sitting about with your toddler in that wee-filled baby pool seems very relaxing but is, in reality, so intensely boring that it drains the life out of you. Because of this paradox, hereby two high-energy suggestions that bring a father back to life:

- Fill the cups: there are two cups on the side of the pool, at some distance from each other. Your toddler stands at the edge of the pool (wearing something inflatable for protection). Her role is to keep the cups empty and your role is to keep them full. Because walking goes faster than swimming, this game is bound to wake you up again.

- Put out the fire: put your child on your back. Scream 'oh no, there is a fire!' and run to the other side of the pool. Upon arrival, the child raises her finger and says 'psss' to put out the fire. She then points to a new fire and off you go again.

Pulling your weight

Children love moving things that seem heavy.
This is why you see children dragging large branches along
on their walks. That same desire helps you in the pool.
You lie on a floating device and she takes your leg or your
big toe, and pulls you up and down the pool. A six-year-old,
pulling the weight of an adult!

And now back to the fountain please

Find the coin

Ask your child to look away and throw a coin anywhere
in the pool. 'Please find it and bring it back to me.' It's
not for crowded pools, obviously, and not for children
who can't swim. For extra relaxation: if you ask
whether you are allowed to watch while
your child tries to find the coin, the
answer is probably an empathic 'NOOO!!'

Taking it on the head

We were in the pool and trying to keep a beach ball in the air. I looked the other way and the ball landed on my head. The children found this funny and a new game was born: 'try to hit daddy's head with the ball.' In this new game, the father's role is reduced to standing in the water, or resting on a floating device, while occasionally getting the ball on the head – which, because the ball is soft and light, feels rather nice. Looking disturbed whenever the ball hits you adds to the merriment.

Assignments

The assignments come to you naturally:

- Guess what I say under water.

- Swim like a dolphin.

- Stand on one hand.

- Exhale and lie flat, on the bottom of the pool.

- Jump up and, as you come down again, make your bottom touch the bottom of the pool.

- Swim upside down under water, through my legs, then jump up as high as possible and push me over.

Initially, I handed out assignments while I floated around on an inflatable tyre. I quickly allowed myself to get dragged into the game and ever since we make up new tasks in turn. It's a lot of fun but once you're part of it, it's no longer relaxing at all.

Ages 6-10 yrs

A note about the next edition

Two or three times per year I write each of my children a letter. I've done this from the moment they were born and will give them all the letters when they reach adulthood. Writing these letters takes time but is very gratifying, and reading them a few years later brings back memories that would otherwise have been lost. (Note the paradox: children grow up so quickly, yet you forget so much of their childhood.)

The letters are all about the things they like and the things they don't, and about the things we used to do together. Writing this book was easy: I extracted most of its contents from these letters.

Perhaps this book's next edition could have less paternal bias and include ideas from other parents, carers, grandparents and child minders. Do you have games and tricks? Please share them with me at willem@totallychilledoutparenting.com

R W
12/15

Acknowledgements

Zena, Amir, Maha, Emma, Gerrit, Roel,
Ida, Saskia, Maarten, Trudi, Hans
and Titus: thanks for playing with me.

Shona, Hans, Petra, Ian, Richard, Marja, Saleh,
Greg, Suzanne and Maarten: thanks for
sparring and for testing things.

Mike: sorry about your shoe (page 33).

*Children complain that the ketchup is touching
their peas; they never complain that life is pointless.
It occurs to me: life never had any meaning, because
it's not a maths puzzle that can be solved.
The secret of life is to play.*

Andrew Clover

If it exists, play with it.

Michael Rosen